Transportation & Communication Series

Television

Kathy Feeney

 Enslow Publishers, Inc.

40 Industrial Road   PO Box 38
Box 398   Aldershot
Berkeley Heights, NJ 07922   Hants GU12 6BP
USA   UK

http://www.enslow.com

Library of Congress Cataloging-in-Publication Data

Feeney, Kathy, 1954-
    Television / Kathy Feeney.
        p. cm. — (Transportation & communication series)
        ISBN 0-7660-1644-7
        1. Television—Juvenile literature. 2. Television—Production and
direction—Juvenile literature. [1. Television.] I. Title. II. Series.
TK6640 .F44 2001
621.388'8—dc21   00-011319

Printed in the United States of America

10 9 8 7 6 5 4 3 2 1

To Our Readers:
We have done our best to make sure all Internet addresses in this book were active and appropriate when
we went to press. However, the author and the publisher have no control over and assume no liability for
the material available on those Internet sites or on other Web sites they may link to. Any comments or
suggestions can be sent by e-mail to comments@enslow.com or to the address on the back cover.

Every effort has been made to locate all copyright holders of material used in this book. If any errors or
omissions have occurred, corrections will be made in future editions of this book.

Illustration Credits: AP Photo, p. 26; AP Photo/J. Scott Applewhite, p. 23; AP Photo/Ed
Bailey, p. 38 (bottom); AP Photo/Bob Galbraith, p. 40 (top); AP Photo/Clark Jones, p. 38 (top);
AP Photo/Jeff Klein, p. 40 (bottom); AP Photo/Mark Lennihan, p. 15 (top); AP Photo/Sabina
Louise Pierce, p. 24; Bettmann/CORBIS, pp. 28, 30, 31; Cecil Stoughton, White House/JFK
Library, p. 4; Corel Corporation, pp. 9, 14, 16, 17, 22, 32, 37; Dover Publications, Inc., p. 20;
Hemera Technologies, Inc. 1997-2000, pp. 1, 2, 5, 6, 7 (top), 11, 19, 21, 25 (top), 27, 33, 36,
39, 41, 42, 43; Hulton-Deutsch Collection/CORBIS, p. 29; Hulton Getty Images, p. 15 (bottom);
Library of Congress, pp. 7 (bottom), 8, 10, 34, 35; NASA, p. 13; National Archives, pp. 12, 25
(bottom); Beth Townsend, p. 18.

Cover Illustrations: Hemera Technologies, Inc. 1997–2000

Contents

4

An Amazing Invention

When the television is off it looks like a blank box. Then click! Someone presses the power button. The television set hums. Its screen lights up. The box is alive with sounds and pictures.

Called TV, television teaches, shows, and tells. People can learn how to build a house, cook a meal, or speak another language by watching TV.

People can see movies, cartoons, or music videos. They can watch the news for tomorrow's weather without leaving their houses.

Television is a great invention. It lets people watch the world outside by bringing it inside. In the 1960s, President John F. Kennedy (center) watches TV from the White House. To his left is Vice-President Lyndon B. Johnson. To the far right is Kennedy's wife, Jacqueline.

Television commercials sell many kinds of products.

The television is a great invention. It has changed lives by bringing the outside world into homes.

The word television comes from two Latin words. *Tele* means faraway. *Videre* means to see. When put together, these words mean "seeing at a distance."

Companies try to sell their products through TV commercials—everything from cereal to shampoo. Companies pay TV stations to show their commercials. The money is used to pay the people who work for the TV station. The money is also used to pay for the shows they make.

Sometimes commercials can be fun to watch. TV commercials show everything from talking washing machines to dancing dogs and cats.

Many commercials are used for important messages. They can tell people where to get help in a time of trouble. Or they can help stop people from using drugs.

Some schools teach classes on television. Students can go to college by watching special shows on TV. Stores use TV cameras and monitors to stop crooks from stealing. Doctors even use tiny TV cameras to see inside the human body.

Many people think TV is the biggest invention of the 20th Century. It could be one of the most popular.

More than 98% of American houses have at least one TV set. That is more than 98 out of every 100 homes!

Many years ago, students watched television to help them learn. Even today, students watch programs that teach them.

Chapter 2

How Television Works

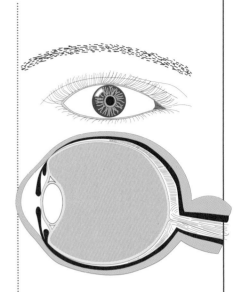

Some people think TV works like magic. But TV needs many parts and people to make the magic happen.

Early TVs had large picture tubes. A picture tube is made of glass. It is curve-shaped and works like the human eye. One end of the picture tube gets an image. At the other end, it turns that signal into a picture.

Once picture tubes were put in huge wooden boxes. This made TV sets big and bulky. The screen was usually the smallest part. As the picture tube and the other parts

Most TV stations send signals through an antenna, like the one seen here (left).

In the 1950s, only some homes had a television. Here, two children watch TV while their father reads a newspaper.

inside the set became smaller, the screens became bigger.

Electronic "guns" inside the TV set shoot out beams to make an image. These guns look like big marking pens. They cannot hurt anyone. The beams they fire stay inside the set.

In the early days of television there were no remote controls. A handle was turned or pulled to turn the set on. People turned a knob with numbers on it to change channels. There were only thirteen channels. Most cities had only seven.

Today TV watchers can channel surf by using a hand-held device called a remote control. It sends a signal to a receiver in the front of the TV set. Buttons pressed on the remote control can turn the set on, change channels, and raise or lower the volume.

Most TV stations send signals through an antenna. It beams the station's signal off of the atmosphere. The signal goes out like an ocean wave, but it cannot be seen. It can only travel a short distance.

A TV set gets signals from a large rooftop antenna or from a smaller antenna on top of the TV set. This indoor antenna is called "rabbit ears."

Cable television is like one long wire connected from the TV station directly to the TV set. The cable company gathers all of

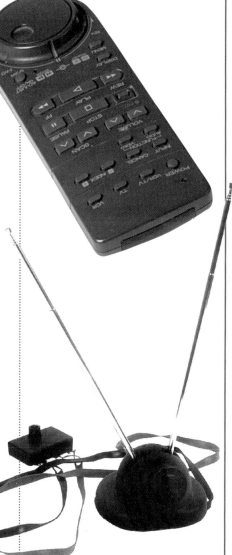

Today people can use remote controls to change the channels on the television.

These are "rabbit ears."

TVs can get their signals from a rooftop antenna.

the channels at one place. From there, the company sends signals through cables that look like long cords. It works much like a telephone line.

Satellite television lets viewers see programs from anywhere in the world. The first TV satellites were made by the National Aeronautics and Space Administration

(NASA) in the 1960s. Satellites are sent out of the atmosphere by spacecraft. NASA's satellites orbit, or circle the Earth to gather information. But TV satellites stay in one spot. Nicknamed "birds," TV satellites are larger than cars.

Satellite TV bounces its signals from space. A signal travels up to the satellite in less than one second. Then the satellite beams the signal back to Earth. Satellite signals are received by a dish-shaped receiver owned by the TV watcher. This receiver is called a satellite dish. Satellite signals provide great pictures.

The different parts of television make it work, but the shows make the audience watch TV. There are many different types of television programs, or shows. They include talk shows, comedies, and dramas. Also, game shows, news programs, and made-for-TV movies.

This satellite is in orbit above the earth.

Television stations also show movies that have already played in movie theaters.

Programs shown from 7 A.M. to 6 P.M. are called daytime programming. Local and world news is sometimes shown between 6 P.M. and 7 P.M. The time between 7 P.M. to 11 P.M. is called primetime. This is when most people are at home and likely to watch a show. Late-night programming is after 11 P.M. Programs

Some talk shows are on TV late at night.

and movies shown, or broadcast, late at night are mostly for adults.

Talk shows are usually aired, or shown, during the day or late at night. Talk shows do not cost as much to make as TV dramas and comedies.

On talk shows the host of the show interviews famous authors, actors, or singers. These people go on the show to talk about their new books, movies, or songs. Many people like talk shows because they are "live." When a program is being broadcast at the same time it happens, it is called "live TV." Live TV lets TV watchers see things as they are at that moment.

Situation comedies are called "sitcoms" for short. Sitcoms try to make people laugh. Sometimes sitcoms are filmed in front of real people so we

Rosie O'Donnell (left) and Oprah Winfrey are popular talk show hosts.

Sitcoms try to make people laugh. *Friends* is a popular sitcom.

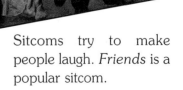

can hear them laugh. Even then, the TV show producers add taped laugh tracks to make it sound like many people are laughing.

Serious TV shows are called dramas. These shows sometimes talk about problems people have.

Sometimes even plays are aired on television.

Most sitcoms and dramas are shown at the same time each week. They are thirty or sixty minutes long, including commercials. Sitcoms and dramas star the same main characters, but the stories change for every show.

Movies made just for TV are called "made-for-TV movies." Movies that run in movie theaters sometimes have bigger stars and cost more to make.

There are two types of network news. They are local and national. News is shown in the morning, early evening, and late at night.

News stations on cable TV can be seen all day. Many news reports are rerun videotapes. A reporter and a cameraperson film the report. Then an editor picks out the best parts. It is the editor's job to make the story the right length. The editor has to decide how important the story is.

This news reporter is talking to a firefighter after a fire has been put out.

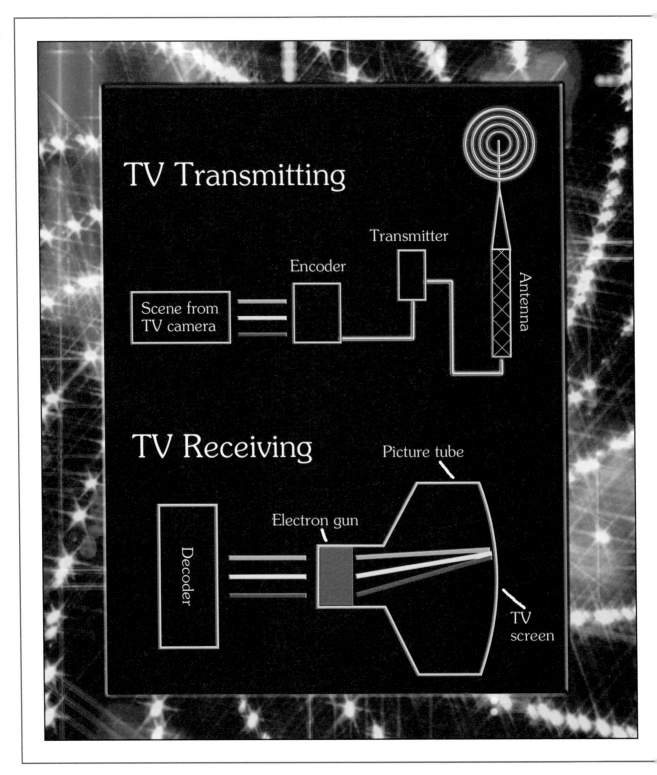

Chapter 3

The History of Television

Before TV, people listened to the radio. Families got together around large wooden cabinets that contained radio sets. People heard comedy and drama programs, music, sports, and news.

Radio audiences had to use their imagination to picture what they heard.

People went to movie theaters to see pictures with sounds. The invention of TV let them be entertained the same way right in their own homes.

The inventors of TV had made working sets by the 1920s.

A scene from a TV camera is broken down into three colors. The encoder turns the three colors into one signal. The signal is then sent to the antenna (top left). Once the signal is received from the antenna, the decoder sends the signal to the electron gun on the back of the picture tube. The electron gun projects the image onto the TV screen (bottom left).

President Franklin D. Roosevelt became the first American president to be on TV.

Americans first had the chance to see television in 1939. It was shown at the World's Fair in New York City.

The theme of the 1939 World's Fair was "The World of Tomorrow." Visitors to the fair watched this amazing new invention called television. It must have seemed like a magical machine from the future.

People squeezed in front of the thirteen tiny TV sets at the World's Fair. Each television was no larger than a toaster. The picture was in black and white. Color television sets had not been invented yet.

During this opening day show at the World's Fair, President Franklin D. Roosevelt became the first American president to be on TV.

Every day visitors at the fair would see and hear something new on TV. They saw baseball games and puppet shows. The fair goers liked television. Everybody wanted one.

But for most people, this new invention cost too much money. Because of World War II, money was needed to make guns and tanks, not TVs.

After the war ended in 1945, many American men and women got married and had large families. From 1946 to 1964, 76 million children were born in the United States. These new families were looking for the easy at-home fun that they could get with TV.

TV sets were not in most American homes until the 1950s. One reason was cost. The first TV sets cost almost as much as cars. In 1940, a car cost about $1,000 and a television set sold for about $200 to $1,000. Another problem was that TV signals were available only to television sets in and near large cities. That meant there were not as many programs to watch.

People watched TV at the one or two houses in the neighborhood that had a set.

In the early years, televisions were too expensive to own. Many people still used their radios to learn about news and sports.

They saw black and white pictures on television sets that received just one or two channels.

Even so, Americans loved television. People wanted to see the pictures that went with the sounds.

On TV, they saw the power of a baseball player's swing. They heard the crack of his bat

People can watch sports on TV. There are some stations that broadcast sports all the time.

hitting a home run. They saw how comedians grinned when they told jokes. TV watchers could see the President of the United States in Washington, D.C., as he talked to them right in their living rooms.

Television has changed the way news is shown to audiences. Before the 2000 election, George W. Bush (center) talks to TV crews. Dick Cheney is to his left and Colin Powell is to his right.

Television changed the way news was shown to audiences. The speed of news reporting became fast. Live 24-hour news has fast updates of world events. There are even TV stations for food, sports, animals, and travel.

Television is used for more than just fun. It can help make homes and businesses safer. TV cameras monitor stores, banks, and office buildings. A security guard can watch an entire building by watching a row of television screens. Security cameras placed throughout the building can identify criminals by catching

The man sitting at the desk is waiting to go on TV. The cameraman is ready.

them on videotape. This kind of TV camera has also helped police officers catch bank robbers.

Both children and adults enjoy playing video games on TV. Sometimes, these games are on separate machines plugged into the TV set. They project graphics onto the television screen. These games offer everything from golf to chess to auto racing and more.

With videocassette recorders, or VCRs, people can record their favorite shows without being at home. A timer on the machine starts recording the show. Then people can watch the program whenever they want to see it.

TV has not totally replaced radio. It has just given audiences a way to see more of the world and hear it, too.

Security guards can watch buildings and even train stations by watching rows of TV screens.

Chapter 4

People Important to Television

These are vacuum tubes.

More than one person invented television. It was made by bringing together the work and ideas of many people. All of their ideas helped to make TV as we know it today.

The beginnings of television go back to 1884 in Germany. That is the year a scientist named Paul Nipkow made spinning disks that could copy pictures. His mechanical scanning machine created an electronic signal. Nipkow then sent the signal to another machine. This receiving machine turned the signal back into the original picture.

From 1921 to 1934, three other men

In 1939, a TV crew broadcasts a baseball game for the first time (top left). A family gathers around a TV in the 1950s (bottom left).

27

Philo T. Farnsworth.

worked separately on television. They were Philo T. Farnsworth of the United States; John Logie Baird of Great Britain; and Vladimir Zworykin, an American citizen who was born in Russia.

Philo T. Farnsworth came up with his theory for electronic television in 1921 at the age of fifteen. One year later he told his high school chemistry teacher about his idea. Farnsworth had a plan to make an electrical system that could capture and project an image.

His machine would be made of two main parts: an image dissector and a cathode-ray tube. Farnsworth's image dissector was a simple television camera. It divided a picture into lines of electricity. His cathode-ray tube was the receiver, or television set. It changed the electricity back into images.

It would take Farnsworth more than ten years to create a workable television machine.

His big break came in 1934. That year Farnsworth showed his machine to the public at the Franklin Institute in Philadelphia. On a 13-inch-wide by 12-inch-high screen, his audience watched dancing bears, dancing humans, and musicians.

His TV display was planned for ten days. But once people heard about Farnsworth's invention, they wanted to see it. So his show went on for 21 days.

John Logie Baird was the first person to televise an image. The year was 1925. One year later, he showed this early television machine to a group of scientists in London. Baird called his invention the televisor. It would become the world's first mass-made television.

By 1928, Baird displayed the first television with color pictures. Color television would take another forty years to be in people's homes.

John Logie Baird.

Vladimir Zworykin made television even better. In 1931, he invented a machine called the iconoscope. This electronic camera tube was the early version of a television camera. He also designed the first kinescope, or picture tube. Zworykin used his iconoscope to send a picture. His kinescope received and recreated the picture. Used together, these machines let him electronically capture images in one place and view them in another place.

Together, the efforts of these inventors helped to make television as we know it today. Large businesses that gave money for more research finally made TV real for most Americans.

This is an early TV camera (left).

Vladimir Zworykin.

Chapter 5

Jobs in Television

A TV station is like a sports team. The players on a television team are called a crew. Each crew member is an important part of the television team.

Visit a television studio and it may look like the crew is rushing around in different directions. Some people yell orders into telephones. Others type quickly on computers. Even though each person is focused on their job, the crew plays together to make a TV show run smoothly and on time.

The producer is like the owner of a sports team. The producer oversees the entire TV

This woman is watching several monitors behind the scenes.

production and controls the money for making the show, or program. Producers are responsible for what a television show is about. This is called content.

A director is the coach of the TV team. A director coaches the crew. The director is responsible for what is seen on TV. The production control room is like the sidelines at a sports stadium. The program's game plan is directed from there. The director decides

A television studio in the 1960s during a quiet time. Most TV studios are busy places.

which camera angles and backgrounds work best.

Sitting behind the control panel, the director watches several rows of TV screens. Each screen is called a monitor. By looking at these monitors the director can coach the crew.

The floor manager is the director's assistant coach. The floor manager works in the studio

The director is the coach of the TV team. This director watches monitors while the cameraman films a scene in the 1940s.

Lots of people work as a team to handle such jobs as lighting, sound, and cameras.

where the action is filmed or videotaped. A floor manager controls what happens on the studio floor.

At the same time, the stage manager also receives directions by headset from the director. The stage manager will pass on these instructions directly to the actors or to the newscasters in the studio.

In another room, sound engineers test the microphones and sound equipment. The sound engineer adjusts the volume of a show and adds background music or sound effects.

People in charge of picture quality and color work in the vision control room. They are called quality control technicians. Without them, the TV picture might not be clear and colors would not look as good.

The people actually seen on TV are called the talent. They include anyone who appears on the television screen. Actors in TV programs and commercials, newscasters,

The people that we see on screen are called the talent. The man in the center is interviewing the man on the right while being filmed.

and game show hosts are some examples. Because they appear on TV so often, audiences recognize them. Maybe that is because they show up in people's homes each day on television.

Behind these stars' familiar faces are many other team players TV watchers never meet. Carpenters build the studio scenery. Costume designers make clothes for actors to wear.

Makeup artists make the talent look good under bright TV spotlights. Electronic technicians make sure the power is connected correctly.

There are musicians, writers, and editors all working together to create an interesting show. Public relations people tell newspapers and magazines when these television shows will appear on TV. Almost all of these background players will never be noticed by the TV audience. But when everybody does their job, the entire television team wins.

TV studios can be in big buildings like this one (top left). Some TV shows have fancy sets, like this one (bottom left).

Lots of people help to put together a TV show.

Chapter 6

The Future of Television

What will TV be like in the future? Bigger and better? Smaller and smarter?

Television screens on the back of airplane seats are already here. Some homes have TVs with large movie theater-like screens. And there are TV sets small enough to carry in a person's pocket.

The biggest change in TV may be how it is used. People can send video messages to a friend's personal TV screen, instead of leaving a voice message on a telephone answering machine.

A video camera in a TV set will send live

This man is holding a new type of remote control. Behind him is a HDTV set (top left).

Using new digital TV technology, some people will soon be able to watch TV on their computer screens (bottom left).

Chef Emeril Lagasse has his own TV show.

In the future, TVs will have sharper pictures and more channels for the viewer to choose from.

messages to a friend and receive messages back. People will print out information they want from television shows. If someone is watching a cooking show, they can print a copy of the recipes.

Television pictures will become even clearer and sharper. TV sets are now available in what is called HDTV. That stands for High Definition Television. HDTV has sharper pictures compared to regular TV. Unlike regular signals, which are called analog, HDTV's digital signals make better pictures.

HDTV is much like looking out an open window. Regular TV is like looking through a window covered by a wire screen. Hundreds of tiny lines create the pictures on the screen. A regular TV screen has about 500 of these lines. HDTV has more than 1,200 lines. More lines make a better picture.

In the future, people will have more choices and control over what they watch. They will be able to watch any show they want at any time. Most cable and satellite broadcasts already offer between 50 to 200 channels. More are being added every day!

Will television in the future make lives easier? A TV with a built-in computer may allow people to shop for groceries, order in pizza, or check on a bank account 24-hours a day just by using the TV's remote control.

Someday TV will respond to human voices. Imagine telling a TV set to turn on or to turn off. Or telling it which type of shows you want to watch and having the TV find them. Or telling it to record movies to watch later.

TV brings the world together through teaching, telling, and showing. People in the future may use television in ways few people today can even think of. The invention of TV was just the beginning of the magic.

Satellite dishes are used to receive TV signals from satellites orbiting in space.

Timeline

1884—Paul Nipkow makes spinning disks that can copy pictures.

1921—Philo T. Farnsworth has plans for electronic television.

1925—John Logie Baird televises an image.

1926—Baird's televisor is the first mass-made television.

1928—Baird displays the first color television.

1931—Vladimir Zworykin invents the iconoscope and the kinescope.

1934—Farnsworth shows his television in Philadelphia.

1939—Americans see television at the World's Fair in New York City.

1940s—TV sets cost a lot of money; Many people do not own TVs.

1950s—Developments in color-television continue; More people own TV sets.

1990s—HDTV becomes popular.

Words to Know

actor—A person or an animal performing in a play, a TV show, or a movie.

antenna—A piece of equipment used to receive radio or television signals.

audience—A group of people who watch or listen to a performance or program.

broadcast—A program that is presented on radio or television.

comedy—A performance that makes people laugh.

cue—A signal used to tell someone what to say or do.

drama—A serious program.

inventor—A person who develops something new.

microphone—A machine that makes sounds louder.

monitor—A screen that shows what is happening in a television studio.

program—A show on television or radio.

studio—A room used to make TV or radio programs.

Learn More About
Television

Books

Davis, Gary W. *Working at a TV Station.* Danbury, Conn.: Children's Press, 1999.

Gibson, Diane. *Television.* North Mankato, Minn.: Smart Apple Media, 1999.

Graham, Ian. *Radio & Television.* Austin, Tex.: Raintree Steck-Vaughn Publishers, 2000.

Lafferty, Peter. *Radio & Television.* Danbury, Conn.: Franklin Watts, Inc., 1998.

Learn More About
Television

Internet Addresses

How Television Works

<http://www.howstuffworks.com/tv.htm>

This site is a great way to find out how a television works with many pictures and diagrams.

Inventors Museum: Inventing Television

<http://inventorsmuseum.com/television.htm>

Learn more about the people who invented television.

Museum of Television

<http://www.mztv.com/worldhome.html>

Visit the virtual gallery of "Television in the World of Tomorrow" to see what TVs used to look like.

Index